A DAY IN THE LIFE OF A
Police Cadet

by John Harding Martin
Photography by Gayle Jann

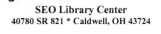

ΓER

Troll Associates

Library of Congress Cataloging in Publication Data

Martin, John Harding.
    A day in the life of a police cadet.

    Summary: Follows a police cadet through his day as he
attends classes in self-defense, CPR, police procedures,
and other aspects of police work.
    1. Police training—New York (N.Y.)—Juvenile
literature. [1. Police. 2. Occupations. 3. Mangual,
Rafael] I. Jann, Gayle, ill. II. Title.
HV7922.M35 1985   363.2'07'15   84-2578
ISBN 0-8167-0103-2 (lib. bdg.)
ISBN 0-8167-0104-0 (pbk.)

10 9 8 7 6 5 4 3 2 1

The author and publisher wish to thank the Police Academy of the City of New York, especially
Captain Robert Alexander and Sergeant Jonathan Evans, for their outstanding cooperation and commitment
to this project.

Rafael Mangual arrives at his job on time, as usual. He is a police cadet, and he can not afford to be late. At the Police Academy of the City of New York, where Rafael is in training to become a police officer, there is never an acceptable excuse for being late. Discipline is the first principle of a cadet's training.

The morning roll call, or "muster," is at eight o'clock. Cadets assemble on the roof of the academy building and listen to instructions from the officer of the day. He tells the cadets that this afternoon they will make a surprise visit to the academy firing range.

Next, the cadets in Rafael's company are inspected by their instructor. He makes sure that they are properly groomed and dressed, and that they are using their notebooks properly. Once the cadets become police officers, their notebooks will be treated as legal records, and may be used in court.

As soon as muster is over, the cadets head for the gym. Physical fitness is a major part of the training program. To graduate from the academy, each cadet must pass strength and endurance tests. Rafael is not a great fan of calisthenics, but he appreciates the importance of this part of his training.

He enjoys self-defense training much more than calisthenics. Often, the instructor works with Rafael to demonstrate new moves to the class. Police officers need to know how to handle themselves in situations where the use of a police revolver would be too dangerous to bystanders.

With his class partner, Rafael practices basic self-defense techniques. They take turns blocking each other's attempts to attack with an imaginary weapon. They also practice how to disarm an attacker. In the streets, a police officer must be prepared for many types of situations.

Next, the cadets work on throwing an attacker to the ground. This requires good timing and coordination. Rafael has learned to overpower someone larger and heavier than himself. He has also learned that a big part of handling himself well is being able to keep a cool head and not to panic.

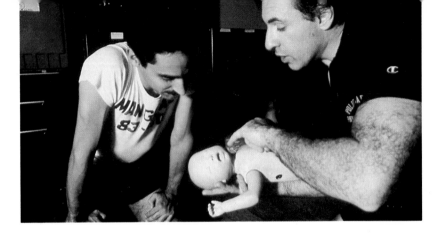

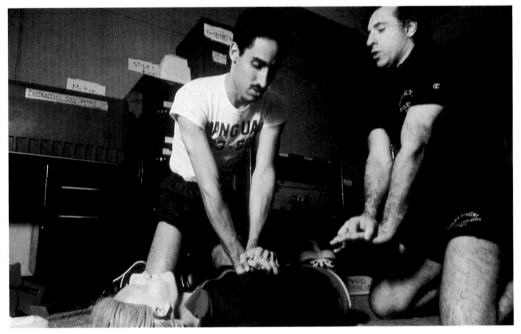

A police officer is often the first person on the scene after an injury or accident has occured. So cadets must learn CPR, or cardio-pulmonary resuscitation. An instructor uses plastic dummies to demonstrate CPR techniques. This training may enable Rafael to later save the life of someone whose heartbeat or breathing has stopped.

In addition to CPR, a police cadet must also master basic first aid. Two of the most important life-saving techniques are stopping heavy bleeding and bandaging severe wounds. The instructor uses a life-size dummy, complete with realistic "wounds," so cadets will not be overwhelmed when they must deal with the real thing.

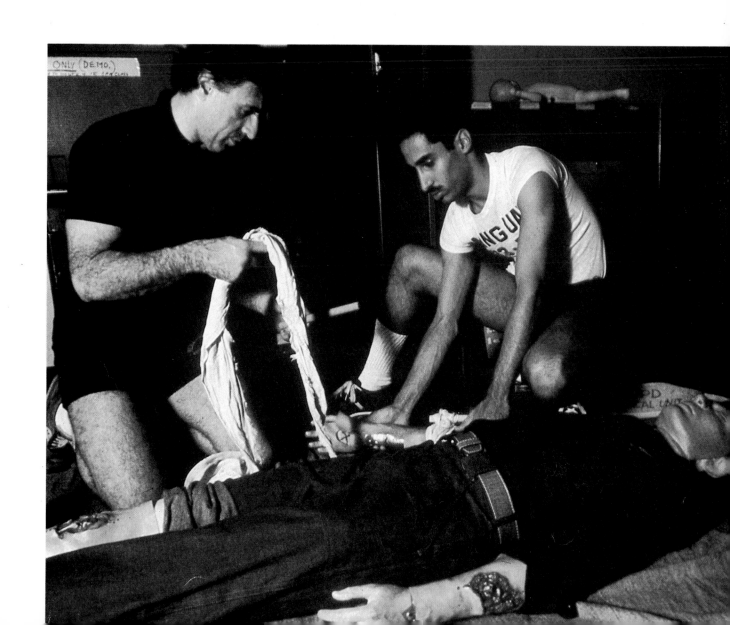

After showering and changing into their uniforms, the cadets move on to their academic classes. A police cadet must learn about police procedures, the law, and society in general. Classroom instruction prepares each cadet for final exams, which must be passed to graduate from the academy.

In one class, Rafael learns how to safely search, or
"frisk," a suspected criminal. Using a plastic gun, he
has the suspect put both hands against the wall and
spread his feet far apart. Then Rafael locates the
suspect's weapon. Failure to find a hidden weapon
could cost a police officer his life.

The "suspect" whose weapon Rafael has found is really an experienced police officer. He points out to the class that criminals have learned many clever ways to hide weapons. He explains that guns come in many sizes, and a thorough frisking of the suspect should always uncover the hiding place.

Next, an instructor explains how to properly fill out a summons. Incomplete information or sloppiness is unacceptable. A major part of a police officer's job is to be neat and precise when doing paperwork. A poorly written summons could cause a judge to dismiss a case when it goes to court.

A police report must also be filled out neatly and properly. It covers all aspects of a police action—date, time, location, circumstances, and identity of witnesses. A police officer keeps the basic information in a notebook, and uses this notebook to fill out the report. Police officers' notebooks are kept for five years in case they are required for use in court.

Before lunch, Rafael and his fellow cadets go down to the garage below the academy. It is time to practice the methods used to stop a car that is believed to be involved in criminal activity. The goal of a "car stop" is to give the suspect no choice but to surrender.

At lunch, the cadets discuss what they learned in class that morning. The academy schedule is so tight that cadets rarely have free time for conversation. Rafael tells how he felt when he almost failed to find the hidden weapon during frisk practice. It is a lesson he cannot afford to forget.

Any time a police officer makes an arrest, the suspect's fingerprints are taken. At a fingerprint workshop, Rafael learns that no two people have the same fingerprints. This makes fingerprints useful for positively identifying people who have otherwise changed their identities. Criminals can change their names, but not their fingerprints.

A police officer depends on a portable two-way radio for communicating with the precinct house. To use his radio properly, Rafael must know all of the special code words that are used. He must also get used to listening to and understanding messages that are sometimes clouded by static.

The Police Academy library, where Rafael often studies during free periods, has a large collection of books and reading materials. Here a police cadet can read about all aspects of police work and the legal system. Raphael's interest goes beyond that of the average cadet. He would like to someday become an instructor at the academy.

The academy firing range is the only place where the cadets are allowed to handle real weapons. At the start of each practice session they review the proper way to load and hold their guns. Cadets are expected to know everything there is to know about the police revolver.

When target practice begins, Rafael fires round after round. He knows that only through practice can he achieve the level of marksmanship for which a police officer strives. He hopes that he will not have to use his pistol often. But it is his responsibility to be as expert a shot as he possibly can.

After the initial round of practice, the company begins "exertion training." First the cadets sprint around the target range, and then follow that exercise with several pushups. The goal is to simulate the exertion of a street chase. Then, nearly exhausted, the cadets must return to target practice.

Although he is breathing heavily, Rafael tries to keep control and fire accurately at the target. The instructor urges him to concentrate, and to learn to put his exhaustion aside. Police officers must often reach deep into their reserves of strength in moments of crisis and danger.

After exertion training, the cadets move on to what is known as the "tactics house." Here they learn the special skills required for capturing an armed and dangerous criminal. They also learn how to deal with a crime that is in progress. The instructor tells them, "Here is the place to make your mistakes, not on the job."

The "crime-in-progress" training requires that cadets be able to act without hesitation. Police officers must develop the kind of instinct that alerts them to danger. The instructor demonstrates how to turn a corner in a dark hallway. The cadets also learn how to react quickly to a dummy that pops out from behind a wall.

Each cadet practices entering a room in which an armed "criminal"—actually an instructor—is hiding. Because the instructor's knowledge of tactics is usually superior to that of the inexperienced cadets, most of the cadets are overpowered. The instructor explains to the entire group each cadet's mistake, and how that mistake can be avoided.

After finishing up in the tactics house, the cadets practice their high-speed driving drills. Police cars are powerful and fast, and the cadets learn how to take them through hard turns. The cadets also learn how to keep the car under control during quick acceleration and braking at high speed.

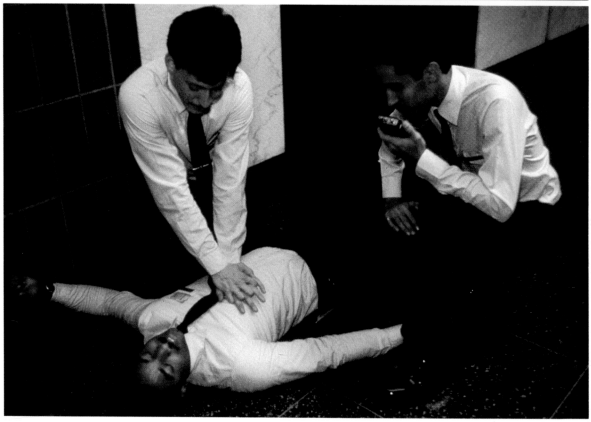

Back at the academy, Rafael and a few fellow cadets take advantage of some rare free time. They rehearse procedures that they are expected to know for their final examination. First, they run through an arrest and the frisking of a suspect. Then they go over the methods used during a CPR emergency, when someone has stopped breathing.

On "Shield Day," Rafael is allowed to wear a police shield and carry a police revolver for the first time. He is proud to have succesfully completed his training at the academy. His lifelong desire to become a police officer is nearly fulfilled.

The next day, before the mayor and the police commissioner, Rafael and 1,300 other cadets graduate from the police academy and officially become police officers. The training at the academy has been hard, and the job of police officer will prove to be even harder. But Rafael has studied hard and trained well, and he is ready.

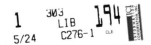